100

THINGS TO DO IN
PORTLAND
OREGON
BEFORE YOU
DIE

100

THINGS TO DO IN
PORTLAND
OREGON
BEFORE YOU
DIE

ANN SMITH WITH ALLISON SYMONDS

REEDY PRESS

Library of Congress Control Number: 2016940399

ISBN: 9781681060545

Design by Jill Halpin

Cover and interior images: Getty iStock

Printed in the United States of America
16 17 18 19 20   5 4 3 2 1

Please note that websites, phone numbers, addresses, and company names are subject to change or cancellation. We did our best to relay the most accurate information available, but due to circumstances beyond our control, please do not hold us liable for misinformation. When exploring new destinations, please do your homework before you go.

DEDICATION

To all of the Oregonians—from the cowboys to the hippies and everyone in between—who have joined me on life's fun ride from the southeast edge of the state to the upper west corner.

• •

CONTENTS

• •

Music and Entertainment

• •

Sports and Recreation

• •

Culture and History

• •

Shopping and Fashion

● ●

PREFACE

City of Roses. P-Town. Stumptown. Rip City. Bridgetown. PDX. However, you refer to it, Portland, Oregon, really is a city like no other. From our obsessions with food, coffee, and microbrews to our passion for soccer, bikes, and the great outdoors, Portlanders pride themselves on not conforming to a standard mold. This book brings to life 100 of our favorite haunts—from the most upscale of restaurants to the diviest of bars; the flashiest of brand stores to the best-kept shopping secrets. Whether you live in town and need a little inspiration or are visiting and looking to explore a lot fast, this collection has something for every mood, appetite, and thrill-seeking threshold. So without further ado, welcome to Portland—and all of its eclectic goodness.

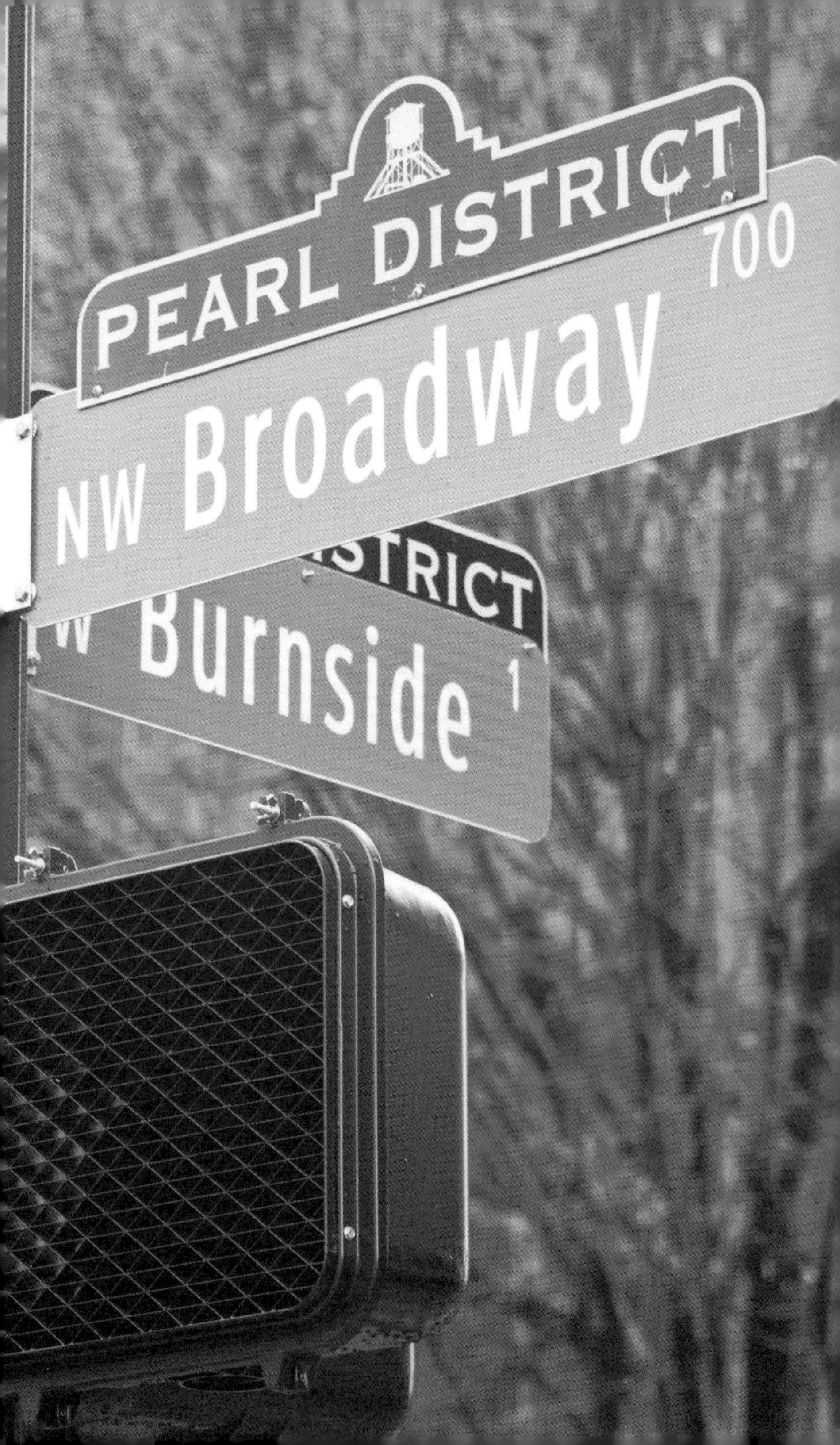
PEARL DISTRICT
NW Broadway 700
STRICT
Burnside 1

ACKNOWLEDGMENTS

Thanks to all of the people responsible for the incredible places and experiences we feature in this book.

To my family and friends for indulging me with weekend morning liege waffles, hundreds of Burncycle rides, and many a pint of Ruby ale.

To Allison for being such a talented, steady force on this project.

And to Portland for never ceasing to amaze.

–Ann Smith

Thanks and love to Josh, who brought me here in the first place.

–Allison Symonds

• •

FOOD AND DRINK

EAT ON THE STREET
FROM A FOOD CART

Some of Portland's highest-reviewed "restaurants" are actually food carts. A fleet of over 600 dot the streets, offering every kind of food you can imagine—authentic Mexican, traditional Thai, grilled cheese, vegan bowls, barbecue, falafel, and everything in between. It's easy to locate the clusters (called "pods") around the city, and you can find online lists of favorites that have become destinations for visitors and locals alike. For the real street food experience, though, explore and experiment on your own. Some have carefully manicured signage, others handwritten menus, but each one's unique. And if you find something amazing, spread the word—you might have found the next big thing in Portland.

DRINK
135-YEAR-OLD COFFEE
AT HUBER'S CAFÉ

Okay, the beverages are fresh, but Portland's oldest restaurant has been serving turkey sandwiches for well over a hundred years. Their signature Spanish Coffee is made with flair, flames, and lots of Kahlúa at your table. But the skilled bartenders are not to be outdone by the wait staff, who give the kind of attention that keeps a business open for a century. Try sitting in the "old dining room," where stained glass ceilings arch over tables. And don't expect anything "fusion." Huber's serves old-fashioned American classics at their best—that tender roast turkey, crisp salads, and fresh Pacific seafood.

411 SW 3rd Ave., Portland, OR 97204
503-228-5666
www.hubers.com

COOL DOWN
AT SALT & STRAW

The brains behind Portland's best-known ice cream shop toe a fine line between brilliant and crazy. You'll find classics like Sea Salt with Caramel Ribbons and Chocolate Gooey Brownie, but adventurous eaters can order a (freshly made) waffle cone with bone marrow, blue cheese, or olive oil ice cream. Whether you're in the mood for sweet and bold or savory and light, they've got you covered. New seasonal flavors are always coming out, but the rich creamy texture and distinct flavors hold true regardless of season. A few licks in, and you'll be on the "Keep Portland Weird" bandwagon.

334 SE Division St., Portland, OR 97202
503-208-2054

2035 NE Alberta St., Portland, OR 97211
503-208-3867

838 NW 23rd Ave., Portland, OR 97210
971-271-8168
www.saltandstraw.com

TIP

Long lines are the norm at Salt & Straw shops,
so impatient ice cream lovers should swing
by earlier in the day.

TOUR THE
JAMES BEARD WINNERS

Portlanders can gush for hours about the city's culinary scene, but the skeptical can turn to the growing list of James Beard notables serving up quality foodstuffs across the city. The prestigious award has elevated these Portlanders to the ranks of food celebrity—here are a few of our favorites.

Cathy Whims
Nostrana, Oven & Shaker, Hamlet

Andy Ricker
Pok Pok, Whiskey Soda Lounge

Gabriel Rucker
Le Pigeon, Little Bird

Naomi Pomeroy
Beast, Expatriate

Greg Higgins
Higgins Restaurant

Vitaly Paley
Paley's Place Bistro & Bar, Imperial,
Portland Penny Diner

Ken Forkish
Ken's Artisan Bakery, Ken's Artisan Pizza,
Trifecta Tavern

HAVE A HAMMERHEAD ALE
AT MCMENAMINS

Enjoying that local beer? Next time, give credit where credit's due and make a trip to one of the many McMenamins destinations around Portland. That's because the city's superior beer scene can be traced back to the McMenamin brothers, who broke ground with the first post-Prohibition brewpub in Oregon in the mid-1980s. Today, the chain has expanded to include breweries, restaurants, hotels, spas, movie theaters, wineries, and concert venues across the Pacific Northwest. The McMenamins make a practice of restoring historic buildings to house their ventures, and they've taken on everything from sagging barns to jails and abandoned school buildings. That means that each one is unique, although you'll spot the murals and much-loved beer list across venues. You can find one in nearly every corner of the city, where it has undoubtedly become a neighborhood favorite. Check out the website and find the McMenamins closest to you.

www.mcmenamins.com

SIP A SACSAYHUAMÁN
(AKA "SEXY WOMAN")
AT ANDINA

There's a rich history associated with the term "Sacsayhuamán," but for now just know it sounds an awful lot like the words "sexy woman," which in turn means the best cocktail in Portland. Made with mango, passionfruit, and habanero-infused vodka, the drink is a must-have on any visit through Portland. Along with a can't-miss happy hour, the restaurant has meshed the unlikely concepts of Peruvian food with vogueish tapas, using fresh, locally sourced ingredients to re-create South American favorites. The resulting menu is both inquisitive and authentic, and the restaurant has been a hit in the competitive Pearl District restaurant scene. The success hasn't gone to their heads though: the bustling room, friendly staff, and flowing liquor create a warm and welcoming ambiance.

1314 NW Glisan St., Portland, OR 97209
503-228-9535
www.andinarestaurant.com

TIP
Order the stuffed pimiento piquillo peppers, beef heart kabobs, and artichokes stuffed with crab from the tapas menu.

TAKE A DRIVE
THROUGH WINE COUNTRY

Small wineries pepper the valleys surrounding Portland, and wine has become an important part of the city's culture. Wine lovers from around the country visit the Willamette Valley for its Pinot Noir, though you'll find a mix of reds and whites across the area. Plan your getaway at a historic bed and breakfast or take a day trip to some of the hidden gems just off the highway. Established vineyards and new start-ups alike have tasting rooms, tours, and great views.

TIP
In between tastings, take the time to explore the area's quirky towns for local culinary favorites, lush scenery, and seasonal fêtes.

TASTE PORTLAND'S
BEST DONUTS

Where? Every Portlander has a favorite, and competition is fierce. Try out a few of the most popular and decide for yourself.

Blue Star Donuts

The dough in Blue Star Donuts is a fried variation on a classic brioche recipe from southern France, but they're anything but traditional. Flavors vary daily, but you can expect elegant, sweet, and unique varieties like bourbon & basil and passion fruit cocoa. Batches are made from scratch every morning, and shops lock up when they've sold out—sometimes as early as noon.

3549 SE Hawthorne Blvd.,
Portland, OR 97214
503-477-9635

921 NW 23rd Ave.,
Portland, OR 97210
503-265-8659

1237 SW Washington St.,
Portland, OR 97205
503-265-8410

3753 N Mississippi Ave.,
Portland, OR 97227
971-254-4575

www.bluestardonuts.com

Pip's Original Doughnuts & Chai

Sweet spiced chai and fresh-to-order doughnuts—what more could you want? Mix and match these mini-doughnuts with a flight of exotic chai varieties and eat to your heart's content.

4759 NE Fremont St.,
Ste. C, Portland, OR 97213
503-206-8692

Sesame Donuts

Sesame Donuts sells delicious, old-fashioned donuts, without the bells and whistles you see at the other destinations on this list. But don't underestimate Sesame, whose familiar, affordable treats have earned a loyal following.

6990 SW Beaverton-Hillsdale Hwy.,
Portland, OR 97225
503-297-8175

727 SW 185th Ave.,
Beaverton, OR 97006
503-372-5829

11945 Pacific Hwy.,
Tigard, OR 97223
503-430-1827

22560 SW Pine St.,
Sherwood, OR 97140
503-217-5170

12700 SW North Dakota St.,
Portland, OR 97223
503-430-1293

2850 NE Brookwood Ave.,
Hillsboro, OR 97124
503-640-3818

Voodoo Doughnut

Expect long lines, and expect to be glad you waited when you dive face-first into a donut covered in bacon, Froot Loops, or gooey chocolate. And if you walk down the street with one of their iconic pink to-go boxes, expect envious stares from passersby.

22 SW 3rd Ave.,
Portland, OR 97204
503-241-4704

1501 NE Davis St.,
Portland, OR 97232
503-235-2666

www.voodoodoughnut.com

Donut Land

My favorite donut shop is tucked away in a nondescript strip mall in the southern Portland suburb of Tualatin. Open early and late, Donut Land is a mainstay for people in its community who come from weekend sport matches and for weekday pick-me-ups. From the traditional maple bar to the killer apple fritter, Donut Land is not to be outdone.

19350 SW Boones Ferry Rd.,
Tualatin, OR 97062
503-885-8641

TIP

Try the cinnamon crunch donut
at Donut Land.

POLISH OFF A STEAK
AT RINGSIDE

I grew up on a cattle ranch, so I can state with some authority that Ringside Steakhouse has amazing steak. This traditional steakhouse is regularly recognized for serving the best beef in the region and offering one of the best wine lists in the country. The dim lighting and tuxedoed waiters are unapologetically old school, and your steak has been cut in-house and aged a minimum of four weeks. If you can, go during Happy Hour, which has become a Portland tradition. Work off the hefty portions with a stroll around historic Nob Hill after dinner.

2165 W Burnside St., Portland, OR 97210
503-223-1513
www.ringsidesteakhouse.com

SEE AND BE SEEN
AT JAKE'S FAMOUS CRAWFISH

Come for the crawdads; stay for the cobbler. Jake's Famous Crawfish is truly a Portland landmark. With a menu chock-full of fresh seafood that is flown in daily, a classic bar, and an atmosphere of sophisticated casualness, Jake's is where to go when you want to feel like you've truly arrived in Portland.

401 SW 12th Ave., Portland, OR 97205
503-226-1419
www.jakesfamouscrawfish.com

SIP A
SWANKY COCKTAIL

A well-made cocktail can make or break a night on the town, so everyone should have a go-to spot. Whether you're sipping a timeless cocktail or a newly inspired invention, you won't go wrong with the temples of mixology below.

Teardrop Cocktail Lounge

As the poshest watering hole in the city's hippest neighborhood, the Pearl District's Teardrop is great for dates, groups, and after-work happy hours.

1015 NW Everett St., Portland, OR 97209
503-445-8109
www.teardroplounge.com

Expatriate

Expatriate draws rave reviews for its attention to detail, exotic decor, and Asian-inspired snacks (try the Indian spiced fries).

5424 NE 30th Ave., Portland, OR 97211
www.expatriatepdx.com

Oven & Shaker

Pair that specialty drink with some memorable wood-fired pizza.

1134 NW Everett St., Portland, OR 97209
503-241-1600
www.ovenandshaker.com

TIP
Order the Pineapple Trainwreck. We dare you to drink just one.

Angel Face

Intimate atmosphere, personalized cocktails, and savory French delicacies. 'Nuff said.

14 NE 28th Ave., Portland, OR 97232
503-239-3804
www.angelfaceportland.com

ADMIRE THE COWS
AT ALPENROSE

For more than a hundred years, Alpenrose Dairy has provided milk, ice cream, and other dairy products to the people of Portland. You can pick up a carton in local grocery stores, but a visit to the farm is an entirely unique experience. Visitors can explore year-round, but Christmas in Dairyville is a delightful family event. Santa Claus, a small herd of "Christmas Cows," and hundreds of volunteers bring this model pioneer town to life throughout the month of December. Make it an afternoon and explore, play, and remember to grab a cone of creamy Alpenrose ice cream.

6149 SW Shattuck Rd., Portland, OR 97221
503-244-1133
www.alpenrose.com

INDULGE YOUR SWEET TOOTH
WITH PORTLAND CUPCAKES

The cupcake trend has spread across the country, but the destinations below are bringing their own Portland spin on the traditional favorite.

Saint Cupcake
1138 SW Morrison St.,
Portland, OR 97205
503-473-8760

3300 SE Belmont,
Portland, OR 97214
503-235-0078

4200 N Williams Ave.,
Portland, OR 97217
503-287-3344

www.saintcupcake.com

Le Cookie Monkey
1902 NW 24th Ave.,
Portland, OR 97210
503-232-3848
ww.lecookiemonkey.com

Cupcake Jones
307 NW 10th Ave.,
Portland, OR 97209

1405 NE Alberta St.,
Portland, OR 97211

503-222-4404
www.cupcakejones.net

Petunia's Pies and Pastries
620 SW 12th Ave.,
Portland, OR 97205
503-841-5961
www.petuniaspiesandpastries.com

Kyra's Bake Shop
599 A Avenue,
Lake Oswego, OR 97034
503-212-2979
www.kyrasbakeshop.com

SNACK ON LATE-NIGHT MAC 'N CHEESE
AT MONTAGE

Le Bistro Montage is the place to go after you've been out on the town, drinking some of Portland's infamous IPAs, and you're ready for some real food. And by real food, we mean real mac 'n cheese. The atmosphere is dark and loud with eclectic décor and custom artwork lining the walls. Even in the dead of night, expect a wait before sitting at one of the restaurant's communal tables. But not to fret, though, as Montage is open until 4 a.m. on weekends. And if your eyes are bigger than your stomach, Montage's wait staff will wrap up your leftover creole mac 'n cheese into one of their best foil animal sculptures.

301 SE Morrison St., Portland, OR 97214
503-234-1324
www.montageportland.com

TRY THE SAUCES
AT FIRE ON THE MOUNTAIN

"Portland's Original Wing Joint," Fire on the Mountain, is a wing-lover's paradise. The restaurant offers everything from traditional wing sauces to unique flavors such as raspberry habañero and buffalo lime-cilantro. Not into chicken? Fire on the Mountain also has great fries, onion rings, and tots, not to mention vegan options for those looking to really mix things up. It's tasty, affordable, and funky—what more does one need when searching out great wings?

4225 N Interstate Ave., Portland, OR 97217
503-280-WING (9464)

1708 E Burnside, Portland, OR 97214
503-230-WING (9464)

3443 NE 57th Ave., Portland, OR 97213
503-894-8973

www.portlandwings.com

CELEBRATE ST. PADDY'S
AT KELLS IRISH FESTIVAL

Run by Belfast transplants, Kells Irish Restaurant & Pub is one of the premier Irish pubs in the Northwest, and it is the place to be on St. Patrick's Day. The revelry overflows from the restaurant into a large tent in their parking lot, where live music, Irish dance, and bagpipes play morning, noon, and night. While the beer is always flowing, daytime events are family friendly. And if you get hungry, don't worry: Kells, whose menu draws praise year-round, keeps serving throughout the event. For the most authentic experience, go see the annual "Kells Smoker," which pits Oregon fighters against Irish Golden Glove boxers. It's definitely the most unique—and raucous—place to celebrate on March 17.

112 SW 2nd Ave., Portland, OR 97217
503-227-4057
www.kellsirish.com

TAKE A TOUR
OF DISTILLERY ROW

Besides the beer and wine innovators that pour up libations in the Portland area, craft hard liquors are making their mark on the local scene too. Many of the most well-known distilleries are located along SE 9th and the surrounding area, known as Distillery Row. In true Portland style, the facilities are pioneering unexpected combinations like rice liquors, spicy spirits made with hot chilies, and specialty fruit-infused liquors. Many offer tours of their production facilities, and inexpensive samplings are an option at most of the destinations for the 21 and older crowd. A Distillery Row "Passport" is even available for brave visitors looking to make the full rounds.

SE Portland, Lower East Side Industrial District
www.distilleryrowpdx.com

GO FOR THE SPICE
AT POK POK

Pok Pok started as a humble food cart; today, it's one of the hottest restaurants in the country. The food is authentic Thai—be prepared for spice—and don't miss the chicken wings, whose crispy outside, tender meat, and salty fish sauce have made them the restaurant's signature dish. Fortunately, the plates are meant to be shared, so you can sample and enjoy a range of dishes with your party. And enjoy people-watching while you eat your papaya salad and noodles, because it's a favorite of Portland's hippest hipsters.

3226 SE Division St., Portland, OR 97202
503-232-1387
www.pokpokpdx.com

TASTE SOME SAMPLES
AT THE BITE OF OREGON

The bounty produced by this big, beautiful state should not be underestimated. Every summer Oregonians from the mountains and the deserts, the coasts and the plains come together to celebrate the state's food, drink, and lifestyle. This festival draws over 50,000 people to the riverfront park in downtown Portland, where a steady stream of live music, family-friendly activities, tastings, and libations keep them entertained. Don't let the revelry confuse you, though, because this is serious business for the food and drink industry. Celebrity chefs hold court over the event, and chefs and mixologists from across the state compete for the titles of Oregon's Iron Chef and Iron Mixologist. You'll regret not taking the chance to join the party and sample the smorgasbord.

Summer
www.biteoforegon.com

THROW BACK
A PINT OF CRAFT BREW

There's nothing like a cool glass of beer on a long summer afternoon; or a dark winter brew beside the fire. Portland has more breweries than any other American city, and our residents are passionate about beer. You'll earn serious street cred by visiting the best.

Cascade Brewing Barrel House

If you've never had them before, the first sip of a sour can be a bit of a shock, so order a line of taster glasses and get acquainted.

939 SE Belmont St., Portland, OR 97214

503-265-8603

www.cascadebrewingbarrelhouse.com

Hair of the Dog Brewery and Tasting Room

Hair of the Dog is known for strong, deep beers with names like Fred, Ruth, and Adam, and offers a special tasting room menu.

61 SE Yamhill St., Portland, OR 97214

503-232-6585

www.hairofthedog.com

Widmer Brothers Brewing Company

A Portland institution, Widmer offers tours of its brewing facilities in addition to a snappy Hefeweizen.

929 N Russell St., Portland, OR 97227

503-281-2437

www.widmerbrothers.com

Hopworks Urban Brewery

If you didn't think a brewery could be family-friendly, guess again. Order a lager while the kids hang out in the play area.

2944 SE Powell Blvd., Portland, OR 97202

503-232-4677

www.hopworksbeer.com

Bridgeport Brewing

Portland's oldest craft brewery also serves great food, from their beloved pretzel plate to a house-made barbeque vegan burger.

1313 NW Marshall St., Portland, OR 97209

503-241-3612

www.bridgeportbrew.com

GRAB LUNCH
AT BUNK SANDWICHES

If you think sandwiches are boring, you haven't been to Bunk. These sandwich shops are serving unusual combos, integrating ingredients like mole, acorn squash, and apple cabbage slaw into their deli menu. The cozy, warm interior at the downtown store leaves little room to stretch out, but their Bunk Bar location on SE Water Avenue can hold a crowd. Go on a sunny day so you can enjoy a frozen margarita while you sit outside with your pork belly Cubano. And keep an eye out for Bunk grub at Timbers games and at the Moda Center, which holds major sporting events and shows.

621 SE Morrison St.,
Portland, OR 97214
503-328-2865

1028 SE Water Ave.,
Portland, OR 97214
503-328-2865

2017 NE Alberta St.,
Portland, OR 97211
503-328-2865

211 SW 6th Ave.,
Portland, OR 97204
503-328-2865

128 NE Russell St.,
Portland, OR 97212
503-328-2865

www.bunksandwiches.com

TIP
If you love meat and peppers, don't pass up the Italian Cured Meats with Marinated Hot Peppers sandwich.

FINISH YOUR CRUST
AT ASH WOODFIRED

Walk along the waterfront near the Ross Island Bridge and you'll stumble upon a food cart pod with the best pizza crust in Portland. Ash Woodfired Pizza's sourdough rises with Oregon yeast and is made by hand daily. Kneaded, hand-rolled to order, and topped with the freshest local ingredients, Ash pizzas are baked to crispy, chewy perfection. The menu changes daily, but you'll always find plain, veggie, and meat options. And unlike many food carts, this one has ample seating. Grab a spot at the picnic table, breathe in the fresh river breeze, and dream of Italy.

3121 SW Moody Ave., Portland, OR 97239
503-941-0196
www.ashwoodfired.com

GET A CAFFEINE BUZZ
ON PORTLAND COFFEE

Cafes are a way of life in Portland. Most of the city's coffee shops are independent, and many have their own cult-like following. The options listed here are only a small sampling of the destinations serving specialty, small-batch brews to discriminating clientele.

Barista
539 NW 13th.Ave., Portland, OR 97209
1725 NE Alberta St., Portland, OR 97211
529 SW 3rd Ave., #110, Portland, OR 97204
823 NW 23rd Ave., Portland, OR 97210

www.baristapdx.com

Heart Roasters
2211 E Burnside St.,
Portland, OR 97214
503-206-6602

537 SW 12th Ave.,
Portland, OR 97205
503-224-0036

www.heartroasters.com

Nossa Familia Coffee
811 NW 13th Ave.,
Portland, OR 97209
503-719-6605
www.nossacoffee.com

Stumptown
Multiple locations
www.stumptowncoffee.com

NOSH
AT KENNY & ZUKE'S

Kenny & Zuke's is raising the bar on deli food everywhere. Where most sandwich dives turn to mass-produced meats and bland bread, owner Ken Gordon is committed to only the freshest, highest-quality ingredients. Oregonians and East Coast natives alike can't get enough of their pastrami, bagels, bialys, knishes, and rye, all cooked fresh every day.

1038 SW Stark St., Portland, OR 97205
503-222-3354

2376 NW Thurman St., Portland, OR 97210
503-954-1737

www.kennyandzukes.com

SAMPLE THE SUDS
AT A BREWFEST

Portlanders are always looking for an excuse to indulge in craft brews, and the city plays host to a variety of top-notch festivals year-round. Some celebrate special varieties like coffee beer and fresh hops; others draw large, diverse crowds from across the region. You'll find brewing tutorials and food pairings, concerts and dancing. But you can always expect great beer and delightfully helpful beer snobs eager to share their craft. A few of the major ones are listed here.

Organic BrewFest
Late August
www.naobf.org

Oregon Brewers Festival
July
www.oregonbrewfest.com

Holiday Ale Festival
December
www.holidayale.com

WALK YOUR PUP
TO LUCKY LABRADOR BREW PUB

The home of Dogtoberfest was one of the first establishments to open its doors to Portland's four-legged patrons. Since then they've become a local staple and a go-to crowd-pleaser. Families and serious craft brew hounds are at home in the cavernous hall, where diners dig into sandwiches, bento boxes, and pizzas of grand proportions. You'll find dogs and their owners nursing Black Lab Stouts on the open patio, which invites slow sipping and easy conversation. The original brew pub is on SE Hawthorne Avenue, but the owners have now opened shop in three other neighborhoods.

Brew Pub
915 SE Hawthorne Blvd., Portland, OR 97214
503-236-3555

Beer Hall
1945 NW Quimby St., Portland, OR 97209
503-517-4352

Public House
7675 SW Capitol Hwy., Portland, OR 97219
503-244-2537

Tap Room
1700 N Killingsworth St., Portland, OR 97217
503-505-9511

www.luckylab.com

A WINDOW INTO THE WORLD
OF WAFFLES

Never underestimate the waffle. The folks at Waffle Window have taken this otherwise unimpressive treat and turned it into a palette of culinary innovation. This unexpected success is literally a window, painted bright blue and flanked by a creative menu of sweet- and savory-topped grid cakes. I waver between the Three Bs and their featured sweet option at any given time—if you just can't decide, splurge and order two! A handful of picnic tables are set up for outdoor dining, or on cold and wet days you might luck out and snag a seat in their limited indoor dining area.

3610 SE Hawthorne Blvd.,
Portland, OR 97214
971-255-0501

2624 NE Alberta St.,
Portland, OR 97211
503-265-8031

7411 SW Bridgeport
(in Bridgeport Village)
Tigard, OR 97224

www.wafflewindow.com

BOTTOMS UP
AT LOCAL DIVES

It might be hard to imagine dive bars thriving in the city that has come to define highfalutin specialty beers, but Portland maintains a healthy scene of seedy watering holes. I promise that these old standbys will leave you satisfied in your search for a dark pub with few windows, greasy food, cheap beer, no-nonsense bartenders, and regulars who have seen it all.

Low Brow Lounge
1036 NW Hoyt St., Portland, OR 97209
503-226-0200
www.facebook.com/lowbrowlounge

Reel M Inn
2430 SE Division St., Portland, OR 97202
503-231-3880

Lutz
4639 SE Woodstock Blvd., Portland, OR 97206
503-774-0353

Kelly's Olympian
426 SW Washington St., Portland, OR 97204
503-228-3669
www.kellysolympian.com

Sandy Hut
1430 NE Sandy Blvd., Portland, OR 97232
503-235-7972

Twilight Room
5242 N Lombard St., Portland, OR 97203
503-283-5091

GET A BITE AND BEVERAGE
AT HAPPY HOUR

If there's one thing nearly every Portlander agrees on (outside of the sacredness of brunch), it's that finding a good happy hour spot to frequent is essential. The city has a wide variety of options, from the fancy to the delightfully dive-y:

Imperial at the Hotel Lucia
410 SW Broadway, Portland, OR 97205
www.imperialpdx.com/happyhour

Rum Club
720 SE Sandy Blvd., Portland, OR 97214
www.rumclubpdx.com

White Owl Social Club
1305 SE 8th Ave, Portland, OR 97214
www.whiteowlsocialclub.com

HOLLYWOOD

HOLLYWOOD

**PORTLAND'S PREMIER
MODERN-HISTORIC MOVIE HOUSE**

**STATE OF THE ART
DIGITAL
16MM 35MM 70MM**

MUSIC AND ENTERTAINMENT

LISTEN
AT JIMMY MAK'S

When someone says "jazz," Oregon isn't the first place that comes to mind. But over the last two decades, Jimmy Mak's has staked out its territory as the best jazz club for miles around. During that time, innumerable greats have jammed inside its dark, curtain-covered walls, and Mel Brown is a regular act. The music's exceptional, the drink selection is great, and there's plenty of space to dance. What more could you want?

221 NW 10th Ave., Portland, OR 97209
503-295-6542
www.jimmymaks.com

BINGE WATCH
PORTLANDIA

Portland has a love-hate relationship with the hit IFC sketch comedy show that both mocks and fawns over our city. But the antics of Fred (Armisen) and Carrie (Brownstein) ring true more often than not, and most locals can quote their favorite episodes. Many have been extras, and even former Portland mayor Sam Adams has a recurring cameo. Once you've caught up on this hilarious ode to hipster culture, take a walk around the city and visit the real-life bookshops, restaurants, and neighborhoods that serve as a natural backdrop to the show.

CATCH A SHOW
AT THE SCHNITZ

What we now know as the Arlene Schnitzer Concert Hall (or the "Schnitz" if you prefer) originally opened to the public in 1928. Over the years, this movie palace has hosted movies, concerts, lectures, and performances of all types, and it is the theater in Portland for the performing arts. Musicians as diverse as Louis Armstrong, ABBA, and Ryan Adams have graced its stage. During the tumultuous period of the 1960s and '70s, the building was at risk of decay and condemnation, but city activists and philanthropists stepped in to return the theater to its original glory. Today, audiences can admire the fully restored Italian renaissance design, complete with graceful sculptures, elaborate castings, multistory French-paned windows, and massive crystal chandeliers. Book tickets for a show, and then arrive early so you can explore the theater's most opulent nooks and crannies, just as Portlanders have done since the early days of American cinema.

1037 SW Broadway, Portland, OR 97205
503-248-4335
www.portland5.com

WATCH A FILM
AT THE PDX FILM FESTIVAL

While more prestigious international film festivals have been running for decades, the Portland Film Festival only held its first season in 2013. But it was a natural addition to the city, which is known for its educated and culturally literate population. The event has quickly received recognition as an outstanding program that delivers a diverse array to discerning audiences. While the festival encourages local talent, it also premieres up-and-coming artists and more recognizable indie talent from around the world. You can catch a show at theaters all across the city, and the event's organizers schedule workshops, speakers, and get-togethers for artists and fans alike. The festival normally runs in late summer, so be sure you keep your calendar open.

www.portlandfilmfestival.com

HO HO HO YOUR WAY
TO SANTACON

To start, let me say that there is no *official* Portland Santacon. At least three major groups pulled out their red suits in December 2015, with unofficial pub crawls sprouting up in neighborhoods across the city. "Anti-Santacons" involving banana costumes occasionally join the fun, and some events are more kid-friendly than others. However, you can expect enthusiastic (but respectful) pub crawls, white beards, and a heavy dose of absurdist Portland camaraderie across the board. It's a quintessential Portland experience, so keep it on your bucket list.

WATCH A MOVIE
AT THE HOLLYWOOD THEATRE

It's hard to miss the Hollywood Theatre's lavish Spanish Colonial Revival facade or the grand marquee suspended over the street. But the facilities inside have been fully updated with a 50-foot screen and high-end surround sound to suit the modern filmgoer. The namesake for the surrounding Hollywood District, the theatre features everything from new blockbusters to Kung-Fu movies and a Hecklevision series. Regional film festivals often make use of the facilities, and you'll always find something fascinating— and usually unique—to watch at the Hollywood.

4122 NE Sandy Blvd., Portland, OR 97212
503-493-1128
www.hollywoodtheatre.org

DRINK KOMBUCHA
AT VELO CULT BIKE SHOP

Portland is a biking city, and literally dozens of bike shops and repair services are available. But none of them are like Velo Cult. It seems there's nothing this destination in Northeast Portland doesn't do. The service and repairs team is brilliant and reasonably priced, and the store sells gear and supplies for casual and expert bikers alike. But Velo stands in its decision to provide everything else. Looking for a place to chill and drink? They've got local beers on tap, a serious tea selection, and kombucha for anyone who can't decide between tea and fermented drink. They have a performance space that regularly hosts local indie bands and karaoke. The shop also supports a local bike team that has a respected presence at events across the state. Thirsty? Bored? Stuck with a broken bike? Velo is your place.

1969 NE 42nd Ave., Portland, OR 97213
503-922-2012
www.velocult.com

GO OLD SCHOOL
AT THE 99W DRIVE-IN

Every time I go to the drive-in, I wonder why this kind of movie-watching went out of style. I'll admit that 99W Drive-In is a bit of a trek, but nothing beats sprawling out on a blanket or lounging in the tailgating seats to take in a summer blockbuster. Many viewers make an evening of it and bring food, cards, and a crew of friends to hang with before the show starts. It feels great to support this family-run business with a visit to the concessions, especially because the ticket price is nothing compared to your friendly neighborhood multiplex. You'll most definitely feel nostalgic at the drive-in, whether you miss the innocent, good old days or are just looking for an excuse to cuddle with your date once the sun goes down. Whatever your motive, this summertime staple belongs on your bucket list.

3110 Portland Rd., Newberg, OR 97132
503-538-2738
www.www.99w.com

TIP
Arrive early because on nice summer evenings the good spots fill up quickly!

BREAK IT DOWN
AT THE CRYSTAL BALLROOM

Ask a group of Portlanders about the Crystal Ballroom, and each one will tell you a different story. That's because this historic event space (now rehabbed and operated by the McMenamins empire) has dabbled in a little bit of everything. Over the years, the roster of artists to grace its stage has included The Decemberists, the Grateful Dead, and Little Richard. The ballroom takes its name from the crystal chandeliers that cascade from the ceiling, but it's the "floating" dance floor that makes it unique. Beloved by both serious dancers and energetic concertgoers, this springy dance surface lets you go late into the night. And when you're part of a crowd of hundreds of people, all dancing, you can't help but join the rhythm. Check out the '80s dance parties or grab tickets to see one of the A-list headliners who pass through the Ballroom's doors.

1332 W Burnside St., Portland, OR 97209
503-225-0047
www.crystalballroompdx.com

LAUGH 'TIL YOU PEE
AT A COMEDY CLUB

Don't let the smug stoicism of Portland's hipsters fool you: we know how to laugh. The city's off-beat mindset, love of beer, and eccentric art scene feed a vibrant comedy culture unlike any other. Though there are smaller options around the city, Harvey's, Helium Comedy Club, the Brody Theater, and Curious Comedy Theater are the big names in town. At any one you can get your fill of open mic, improv, and stand-up performances from local and visiting comedians. Don't miss the Bridgetown Comedy Festival either, which attracts entertainers from across the country to Rip City. Wherever you go, you'll find warm, enthusiastic crowds, copious beer, and plenty of laughs.

Brody Theater
16 NW Broadway, Portland,
OR 97209
503-224-2227

Helium Comedy Club Portland
1510 SE 9th Ave., Portland,
OR 97214
1-888-643-8669
www.portland.heliumcomedy.com

Curious Comedy Theater
5225 NE Martin Luther King Jr.
Blvd., Portland, OR 97211
503-477-9477
www.curiouscomedy.org

Harvey's Comedy Club
436 NW 6th Ave., Portland,
OR 97209
503-241-0338
www.harveyscomedyclub.com

Bridgetown Comedy Festival
www.bridgetowncomedy.com

SPORTS AND RECREATION

ROOT FOR
THE PORTLAND THORNS

In the City of Roses, the Portland Thorns aren't afraid to draw blood. These fierce competitors make up Portland's professional women's soccer team, which plays through the mild spring and summer months. The stadium fills up with fans eager to watch some of the best talent from around the world, many of whom have made appearances in recent FIFA Women's World Cups. Beating drums drive the festive atmosphere, but the crowd needs little urging. Great beer and nearby food carts are an added bonus.

www.timbers.com/thornsfc

HIKE THE
EAGLE CREEK TRAIL

Located on the Oregon side of the Columbia River Gorge, Eagle Creek Trail is one of the most popular hikes in the area, after the Multnomah Falls trails. The trek is a breathtaking (and occasionally heartpounding) hike not for the faint of heart. Early trailblazers blasted a path into the cliffside, leaving steep drops and narrow passings for today's hikers. But the payoffs are serious and can't be matched—dazzling waterfalls, moss-covered trees, and slender bridges highlight the route. If you're feeling weary, take a break and go for a dip in the chilly Punch Bowl to refresh yourself mid-trek. Hikers can choose between two different trails—a moderate 4.2-mile trek or a difficult 12-mile journey for the more adventurous.

Trailhead is at NE Eagle Creek Loop, Portland, OR 97203.

TAKE A RIDE
ON THE *PORTLAND SPIRIT*

You haven't truly experienced Portland until you've seen it from a riverboat, and the city's history is inextricably linked to the rivers that flank it. The earliest American explorers arrived by boat, and since then ships, canoes, and everything in between have held an essential place in the heart of the city. The *Portland Spirit* is a 150-foot yacht now open to the general public. Dining on a historic boat inspires an atmosphere of old-world charm, but the boat also offers modern, high-end cuisine, dances, cruises, and special events. During the winter holidays it hosts celebrations for families, and it marks other special occasions seasonally. Once you admire the landscape and city lights while cruising down the river, you'll never wonder again why those explorers stopped here.

503-224-3900
www.portlandspirit.com

WEAR A COSTUME
TO THE SOAPBOX DERBY

Every summer, skilled and amateur teams race, roll, and putter their way down Mt. Tabor for the Adult Soapbox Derby. The contraptions rarely resemble cars (or karts, for that matter), but speed is not the objective in this event. Drivers wear nonsensical outfits, and some of the most prestigious prizes are awarded in the categories of Fan Favorite, Shit Talker, and Best Costume. The event is fueled by craft beer, and roaring crowds cheer on their favorite buckets of bolts. Relatively unknown to out-of-towners, this event embodies all things Portlandia.

Mt. Tabor
August
www.soapboxracer.com

PORTLAND INTERNATIONAL
RACEWAY

Cars are a ubiquitous American universal, and they draw fans of all shapes and sizes. Perhaps that's why catching a race at the Portland International Raceway is such a thrilling experience. The track hosts nearly everything car- and race-related: they have vintage shows and races, rally, autocross, drag, road racing, and motocross. This city-owned facility was designed to optimize watching points, whether you're eyeballing the cars or the car enthusiasts. Rednecks, retirees, car junkies, and auto connoisseurs all converge at the track, where the top speed was clocked at 324.90 miles per hour. Spend an afternoon in the crowd, or visit during seasonal and holiday events throughout the year.

1940 N Victory Blvd., Portland, OR 97217
503-823-7223
www.portlandraceway.com

・・・・・・・・・・・（ **45** ）・・・・・・・・・

GO FOR
A RUN DOWNTOWN

Experience Portland in a new light when you participate in one of the many local foot races that take over the city on weekend mornings. Downtown Portland is a great place to chill during the day, but it's an entirely different experience when you're taking in the view as you trot over a bridge in the early morning. And these aren't just jogs—Portland's coolest runs support important causes, sport silly themes, or mark special events. Put on a costume and run along the riverfront; cool off after a 10k with a local brew; or gear up to sweat your way through a sea of green on St. Patrick's Day. Just a few of my favorites are listed below.

Race for the Cure
www.komenoregon.org

Shamrock Run Portland
www.shamrockrunportland.com

Bridge to Brews
www.terrapinevents.com/bridge-to-brews

Rum Run (rum + run = winning)
energyevents.com/rum-run-registration

61

ESCAPE TO
SAUVIE ISLAND

This awkwardly stationed island just downriver of Portland remains relatively uninhabited, as most of it is occupied by family farms or a state park. It is, however, a beloved destination for many Portlanders to visit. Birdwatchers and hikers scramble along the banks to reach an active lighthouse, and the sandy riverfront is the closest thing to a beach for a hundred miles. Depending on the season, you may run into summer crowds gorging themselves on U-pick berries, and it is a top destination for pumpkin pickers come Halloween. Don't forget to purchase a pass for your car so that you can park on the island, which has only a single gas station and few other urban amenities. Feeling in the mood to let it all hang out? Sauvie Island also sports a clothing-optional beach called Collins Beach—a popular spot for nudists since the 1970s.

PRETEND YOU'RE SUPERMAN
AT IFLY

There's something admirable about a company whose goal is "to make the dream of flight a reality" for the masses. iFLY offers an indoor skydiving experience that's safe, inexpensive, and just down the road, in Tigard, Oregon. Guests as young as 3 (and as old as 100) get hands-on training and instruction with experts before taking their turn in a vertical wind tunnel. Show off and ride the adrenaline rush while floating, flipping, and turning in midair—and then cross a big-ticket item off your bucket list.

10645 SW Greenburg Rd., Portland, OR, 97223
971-803-4359
www.iflyworld.com/portland

LOOK FOR LEPRECHAUNS
AT MILL ENDS PARK

To see Mill Ends Park, you have to lean in close. The official boundaries occupy a circle just two feet in diameter, making it the world's smallest park. Dedicated in 1948, the circle is tucked in a road median halfway across a SW Taylor Street downtown. Over the years it has been the site of protests, flowers, shrubbery, and butterfly pools. Today, a small tree occupies much of the space and provides a natural habitat for the leprechauns who call the park home. The leprechauns are shy, but if you're lucky you may be able to catch a glimpse of one.

SW Taylor St. and Pacific Hwy. W, Portland, OR 97204

FLEX YOUR HAMSTRINGS
IN THE PORTLAND MARATHON

No one's ever described a 26.2-mile run as easygoing or quaint, but if they did they'd be talking about the Portland Marathon. The annual road race meanders through cute neighborhoods, where onlookers cheer runners on by their first name (conveniently printed on their bib) and across spectacular bridges. Participants can enjoy ongoing live entertainment along the course, and because it's held in October, the weather is often cool and comfortable. And while the race is competitive, runners are warned that they may need to slow down for the occasional train.

www.portlandmarathon.org

FEEL THE SPRAY
FROM MULTNOMAH FALLS

It's no Niagara, but Multnomah Falls draws 2 million visitors a year, making it the most popular recreation site in the Pacific Northwest. The cascade has awed tourists and locals for centuries, and it is easily accessible for even the most casual visitor. Admire the steep drop from the bottom, and then make the short walk up the footbridge to feel the mist upon your face. The crossing is a favorite photo site and a prime opportunity to use your selfie stick. But don't stop at Multnomah. The Columbia River Gorge has several other beautiful (and only slightly less impressive) waterfalls, some visible from the roadway, others only accessible by foot.

LIVE
LIKE A DOG

Portland is a dog-loving city. Pull out the leash and explore the best
the city has to offer for canines and their owners.

Sellwood Riverfront Park
Great off-leash area alongside the Willamette
SE Oaks Park Way, Portland, OR 97202

Salty's Pet Supply
Boutique pet shop in North Portland
4039 N Mississippi, #104, Portland OR 97227
503-249-1432
www.saltyspetsupply.com

Tin Shed
Café with a menu for your dog too
1438 NE Alberta St., Portland, OR 97211
503-288-6966
www.tinshedgardencafe.com

WATCH THE SWIFTS
AT THE CHAPMAN SCHOOL

The diminutive, agile Vaux Swift sustains itself on bugs and insects. It also migrates, annually, from the northern extremes of North America all the way down to Venezuela. In late summer, that route passes right through Portland, where they zoom around by the thousands. The birds traditionally sleep in hollowed-out Douglas firs, but today's environmental reality has made chimneys the resting place of choice for many. Since the 1980s, the chimney of Chapman Elementary School in Northwest Portland has become their largest gathering spot. The chimney is no longer operational, so local bird lovers make their own annual pilgrimage to ooh and ahh as the winged wonders zip around in the evening sky. It's a sight unlike any other and a relaxing but thrilling way to enjoy a summer sunset.

The Chapman School
1445 NW 26th Ave., Portland, OR 97210

CHEER FROM SECTION 107
AT A TIMBERS GAME

Professional soccer may have trouble getting a foothold in the US, but the Portland Timbers have sold out every home game to date. The self-styled Timbers Army, the franchise's most enthusiastic fan group, has grown steadily in recent years. This boisterous group occupies section 107 of Providence Park, where they wave carefully orchestrated tifos, set off green smoke bombs, and lead the rest of the park in chants. Games against chief rival the Seattle Sounders are particularly exciting, but there's never a dull seat in the house.

www.timbers.com

TIP
Wear or buy a green Timbers scarf –
it's the ultimate statement of Portland pride.

BOWL A STRIKE
AT GRAND CENTRAL BOWL

It seems no one at Grand Central Bowl got the memo that bowling alley food is supposed to be, well, gross. Visit this entertainment mecca on Southeast Morrison and sink your teeth into seared Ahi salad or a blackened Cajun burger. Drink a craft beer between strikes. And when you've finished enjoying the upscale bowling alleys, head upstairs. The second level houses an awesome arcade, with everything from air hockey to Dirty Driving video games. The place is an awesome destination for groups, parties, or a night on the town.

808 SE Morrison St., Portland, OR 97232
503-236-2695
www.thegrandcentralbowl.com

FROM HOOD
TO COAST

"The Mother of All Relays" is a far cry from the baton races you ran in third grade. Every year, hundreds of teams participate in this 198-mile run as a trial of endurance, temperature, and sanity. Starting at Timberline Lodge, at an altitude of 6,000 feet on Mt. Hood, runners divide the trek into 36 legs, which travel down the mountain, across the northwest corner of the state, and all the way to the beachside town of Seaside, Oregon. About a third of the way in, the runners reach Portland, where they cross the Hawthorne Bridge and stride through downtown before hitting the hilly roads to the Oregon coast. Runners come from far and wide to be part of this annual event. But if you're more inclined to cheer from the sidelines versus lacing up your Nikes, you can do so by camping out and cheering at the designated handoff spots, or finding a view along the route.

www.hoodtocoastrelay.com

CATCH A ROSE CITY
ROLLERS BOUT

With over 400 strong, skilled female athletes across nine squads, the Rose City Rollers challenge stereotypes about what it means to be a woman in sports. The women on the roller derby teams range in age from 7 to 60, and are shining examples of confident, tough athletes. Their games are also a seriously fun time for fans—it's a fast-paced, inclusive sport and just generally a great way to spend an afternoon. The 22,000+ fans who attend bouts throughout the year can't be wrong.

www.rosecityrollers.com/events

TAKE A RAINY DAY HIKE
IN FOREST PARK

Oregon has some of the most stunning old-growth forests in the country, but you don't have to leave the city limits for a hike in the woods. Over 80 miles of trails crisscross the eastern slope of the Tualatin Mountains northwest of downtown, which includes bike routes, footpaths, and fantastic bird-watching. Even on drizzly days, the lush moss and bubbling creeks provide a welcome respite from urban life—but you'll never be far from a pint of craft beer.

www.forestparkconservancy.org

CHEER ON THE PORTLAND TRAIL BLAZERS
AT A HOME GAME

Portland is a city of many nicknames, but one of the most distinct is "Rip City." Coined by legendary announcer Bill Schonely during the Portland Trail Blazers' first season in 1971, Rip City has grown into a loyal fan base that packs the Moda Center during every home game. The Trail Blazers rank in the top 10 NBA teams for home game attendance, with an average of almost 20,000 fans cheering them on each time. Be sure to check out the hype at a home game for the Pacific Northwest's only professional basketball team.

www.nba.com/blazers

GET SOME INSTAGRAM-WORTHY SHOTS
ALONG TOM MCCALL WATERFRONT PARK

Portland's picturesque quality is all the more apparent as you're strolling along the Willamette River and watching cherry blossom petals flutter by. Tom McCall Waterfront Park offers a trail parallel to a large span of the river dotted with great spots for a picnic or photo shoot. The views of several of the city's bridges are fantastic, and the trails pass by several Portland landmarks, including the Portland Saturday Market and the Oregon Maritime Museum. Many popular dinner spots are close by. You can also find dinner cruises, concerts, and fun boutique hotels along the park.

BOUNCE, SPLASH, AND RACE
AT THE CHILDREN'S MUSEUM

Before entering the Portland Children's Museum, prepare yourself for the explosion of joy inside. From 9 a.m. to 5 p.m. every day, the building is full of happy, smiling, laughing families. Kids experiment with shadow, light, and color in an indoor forest. Toddlers clamber over boulders and splash in water tables. Children save stuffed animal lives at the pint-sized veterinary clinic and race wooden trains in the "Vroom Room." Parents watch their young ones in DIY productions on stage. There's far too much to see and do for one visit, so you might need to rally the family for multiple trips. When the weather's right, make sure to get your fill of their engaging outdoor area.

4015 SW Canyon Rd., Portland, OR 97221
503-223-6500
www.portlandcm.org

TIP
Keep an eye out for new temporary exhibits.

TAKE A RIDE
IN A HOT AIR BALLOON

What, you didn't think the Willamette Valley could get any more stunning? Nothing—absolutely nothing—can compare to the spectacular view of the landscape from hundreds or thousands of feet in the sky. Vista Balloon Adventures, operating just 30 minutes southwest, in Newberg, is one of Portland's best-kept secrets. Their capable guides are experts at pointing out vineyards, rivers, farms, and woodlands below, dipping down for water landings, and calming nervous fliers. Flights rise early in the morning when the air is still cool, and afterward they serve a catered brunch on the ground. It's unbeatable as a romantic getaway or family adventure, and I promise you'll get a whole new look on life—or at least of Oregon.

Vista Balloon Adventures, Inc.
April through October, weather permitting
1050 Commerce Pkwy., Newberg, OR 97132
503-625-7385
www.vistaballoon.com

PICK A PECK
OF PUMPKINS

Come October, Portlanders bust out the costumes, cider, and corn mazes with full force. Check out one of these pumpkin patches to get a taste of the fun.

TIP

Roloff Farms is owned by the family featured in
TLC's *Little People, Big World*.
If you're lucky, you might run into a couple reality TV stars.

Kruger Farms
Sauvie Island
17100 NW Sauvie Island Rd., Portland, OR 97231
503-621-3489
www.krugersfarmmarket.com

Roloff Farms
23985 NW Grossen Dr., Hillsboro, OR 97124
503-647-2899
www.therolofffamily.com/farm

The Pumpkin Patch
Sauvie Island
16511 NW Gillihan Rd., Portland, OR 97231
503-621-3874
www.thepumpkinpatch.com

Baggenstos Farm
15801 SW Roy Rogers Rd., Sherwood, OR 97140
503-590-4301
www.baggenstosfarms.com

SKI THE SLOPES
OF MT. HOOD

On clear days, you can see five snowcapped peaks from Portland. But Mt. Hood is nearest and dearest to Portland's heart. As the highest point in Oregon (at 11,240 feet), it's one of the state's most recognizable and beloved landmarks. This (sleeping) volcano rises from the Cascade Mountains just 50 miles outside of the Portland city limits. Depending on the time of year, you'll find hikers, skiers, showshoers, snowboarders, and serious mountain climbers along its slopes and in the surrounding National Forest. Pack up your gear and make it a day trip, or stay at one of the cozy ski lodges—most notable Timberline Lodge—that surround the peak.

WALK UNDER THE ARCHES
OF CATHEDRAL PARK

Cathedral Park's most identifying feature is not what's in the park, it's what's above it. This riverfront park occupies the space under and around the St. Johns Bridge, whose gothic arches give this stretch of grass its name. The park is a favorite with dog owners, who love the off-leash area beside the river, and a floating dock marks the waterfront. Pleasant walking trails, grassy patches, and lush trees draw walkers and picnickers on a daily basis, and the St. Johns neighborhood is actively involved in the park. Visitors come from across the city, however, for the annual Cathedral Park Jazz Festival during the summer.

N Edison St. & Pittsburg Ave.
www.portlandoregon.gov/parks

SPEND A DAY
AT THE RACES AT PORTLAND MEADOWS

Never been to a horse race in your life? Portland Meadows is the perfect place to start. The city's track sits in an industrial section of North Portland, and the facilities are a little tired, a little outdated. But it still has an active racing culture, and it's a great place to dive into the horse racing world. You can place small bets at the desk, use the betting machines, or just observe the old-time regulars intently choosing their picks with pencils and newspapers in hand. The Turf Club has an exceptional brunch, and the track's bar can't be beat. Grab your drink and venture outside, where there's ample seating to watch the region's top horses give it their best.

Portland Meadows
1001 N Schmeer Rd., Portland, OR 97217
503-285-9144
www.portlandmeadows.com

HIKE TO THE TOP
OF MT. TABOR

Climbing volcanos is not an everyday activity for most people, but the residents of Portland have one in their front yard. Don't worry though, Mt. Tabor is certifiably dormant for the foreseeable future. That makes it a perfect destination for hikers, walkers, bikers, friends, parents, children, couples, picnickers, sledders, dogs, basketball players, yogis, concertgoers, runners, LARPers, tennis players, and skateboarders. It's also the site of historic and beautiful reservoirs for the city of Portland. Take a walk up to the summit, where you'll discover dozens of Portlanders reading, playing, and admiring the magnificent lookout over the city.

SE 60th Ave. & Salmon St., Portland, OR 97215

BURN,
BABY, BURN

Step into darkness, surrender to the beat of the music, and get ready for the ride of your life at Burncycle. Deemed whole body cycling, Burncycle is more than just a workout, it's an emotional release complete with plenty of sweat, cheers, and high fives. Classes are 45 minutes long and held throughout the day in both of Burncycle's Portland studios. Led by some of the most motivational (and ridiculously fit) people you'll ever meet, the rides feature a range of runs, climbs, and upper body choreography. Founded by Portland "Boss Lady" Jessi Duley, Burncycle has created a rabid following (known as the BURN Army) of mothers, hipsters, men, and everyone in between who are looking to crush it on an indoor bike. Don't be surprised if you see Burncycle enthusiasts riding outside of the studios either; bikes are known to pop up everywhere, from BURN's own Portland Pride Fest float to rooftops and Bridgeport Village. Classes can be reserved online—but don't wait…the most popular instructors' rides fill up in a matter of minutes!

910 NW 10th Ave.
Portland, OR 97209
503-946-8618

4811 Meadows Rd., Suite 109
Lake Oswego, OR 97034
503-303-4169

www.burncyclepdx.com

CULTURE AND HISTORY

START
YOUR WEEKEND EARLY
AT FIRST THURSDAY

On the first Thursday of every month during the summer, the Pearl District lets its hair down. The art galleries of this Northwest Portland neighborhood open their doors and invite the hoi polloi in to admire (and hopefully purchase) the products of Portland's creative class. Many offer free food and drink, and artists are frequently on hand to engage with patrons and share their creations. The major showrooms along Flanders Street headline the evening, but smaller storefronts and street-side creators also peddle their wares. You'll see everything from more conventional paintings and sculptures to innovative photography and provocative conceptual art. On pleasant evenings the streets are filled to the brim with visitors, so take your time and people watch as you stroll.

The Pearl District
www.firstthursdayportland.com

COUNT
THE BRIDGES

Portland loves its nicknames. And while the origins of "Rip City" or "City of Roses" may make little sense, it's obvious why the city is known as "Bridgetown." Situated at the meeting point of the Columbia and Willamette Rivers, Portland has found creative ways to straddle the banks since its founding. The city has a total of 12 major bridges, each unique in its own way. Some are graceful, some are boxy, some offer passage to bikes and pedestrians, and others serve as parts of Highway 405. If you're feeling ambitious, start at the iconic St. Johns Bridge to the north, work your way down the Willamette, and then across to the Columbia to count them all.

TIP
Extra credit if you make it to the Sauvie Island Bridge
or any of the crossings south of the city.

WATCH DOWNTOWN'S
BIGGEST PARADES

Street life in Portland pushes the limits no matter what the season, so when downtown closes the roadways for a parade, we pull out all the stops. Each of the events below is a must-do for your summertime bucket list.

LGBTQ Pride Parade
Seventy thousand visitors can't be wrong. Locals
and out-of-towners, LGBTQ and allies, show up
in massive numbers for this legendary celebration,
and the parade is the highlight of the event. Try to
snag a prime spot so that you can take in the view as
Portland's proudest strut through downtown.
www.pridenw.org

The Grand Floral Parade
The main display at Portland's iconic Rose Festival
showcases extravagant, colorful floats spaced by
marching bands, horses, and other groups. Expect a
classic American parade decked in thousands
and thousands of flowers.
www.rosefestival.org

The Starlight Parade
Unlike your average city festival, the Rose Festival has
two parades. Not to be outdone by its more traditional
companion, the Starlight Parade has slotted itself as
a funky, nighttime display of glow-in-the-dark and
illuminated entries sponsored by community
groups across the city.
www.rosefestival.org

HAVE A PICNIC
AT THE PITTOCK MANSION

Be transported back in time with a visit to the Pittock Mansion, a historic estate overlooking the city. The house itself is visually magnificent, and tickets are available to explore the inside. Take your time with a self-guided tour of the opulent rooms and fascinating 1910s technology. The Pittock family ran an empire of newspapers, agriculture, and industry, so the place is chock-full of family and Portland history. And don't forget to explore the grounds. The lookout is arguably the most spectacular view of the city, and on clear days you can pick out several snowcapped peaks in the background. Adventurous (and athletic) visitors can hike up to the house along steep, wooded trails, and during the summer the lawn is a great place to spread out a blanket and have lunch.

3229 NW Pittock Dr., Portland, OR 97210
503-823-3623
www.pittockmansion.org

CHANNEL
YOUR INNER CHILD
AT OMSI

Do you ever wish you could play the way you did when you were a kid? Your visit to the Oregon Museum of Science and Industry is your chance. Lean back and take in the planetarium, discover hydrodynamics (aka, splash on a water table), and experience weather patterns from inside a six-foot sphere. The life sciences hall will walk you from the states of human fetal development to the process of old age. The highlight of the museum is the USS *Blueback,* a decommissioned military submarine from the 1950s (and a minor movie star for her role in the 1990 movie *The Hunt for Red October*). Your tour guide—a sub veteran—will guide you through the cramped, condensed world of submarine living, and you can peek through the periscope while learning the laws of submersible mechanics. Visit during the daytime and watch the packs of children engage in interactive learning, or go in the evening for one of the adults-only gatherings.

1945 SE Water Ave., Portland, OR 97214
503-797-4000
www.omsi.edu

EXPERIENCE SERENITY AND HUSTLE AND BUSTLE
IN CHINATOWN

Want to get the most Portland you can in one afternoon? Head to Old Town Chinatown. You'll find some of the best shopping in the city at the Portland Saturday Market while taking in unique, historic architecture. It's also home to the world-famous Voodoo Doughnut and the Ground Kontrol Classic Arcade. For a change of pace, stop in the Lan Su Chinese Garden. Created and maintained with materials shipped directly from Suzhou, China, the garden is one of the most authentic Chinese gardens in the US and offers a little bit of quiet in the heart of the city.

MEDITATE
AT THE GROTTO

At first glance, The Grotto is an unlikely attraction. Officially known as the National Sanctuary of Our Sorrowful Mother, this refuge at the eastern limits of Portland is, above all, a Catholic shrine. But it's beloved among worshippers and non-believers alike for its beauty and serenity, and people from all walks of life are welcome. A cave containing a replica of Michelangelo's *Pietà* is the sanctuary's focal point, and it's usually flanked by glowing candles and fresh flowers. Pensive visitors meander through gardens filled with blossoming bushes, soaring trees, and marble statues. An elevator rises to the top of the cliff, where the nature is equally as beautiful and the vista even more so. Visit for a pleasant afternoon, or make it a regular stop on days when you need a break from the real world.

8840 NE Skidmore St., Portland, OR 97220
503-254-7371
www.thegrotto.org

TIP
Turn off your phone before you enter—
this one is best enjoyed "unplugged."

GO WHALE WATCHING
AT THE PORTLAND ART MUSEUM

The indigenous coastal communities of the Northwest celebrated whales everywhere in their art and designs. The Portland Art Museum features eye-opening collections of these artifacts, which will make you see Oregon in an entirely new light. And the Northwestern collections are accompanied by beautifully detailed clothing, bags, tools, and other lifestyle items produced by native peoples across North America. Contemporary native art and photography also fill gallery walls, and guests can track Northwest art from the pioneer days into today. But this isn't just a museum of Native American art. You'll also find beautiful prints from name-brand European masters, rich Asian art collections, and intriguing contemporary art. Visiting exhibits change seasonally, so there's always something new to see.

1219 SW Park Ave., Portland, OR 97205
503-226-2811
www.portlandartmuseum.org

EXPERIENCE
THE HAWTHORNE DISTRICT

The Hawthorne neighborhood epitomizes everything Portland is known for: quirky, unique, a little bit hippie and a little bit hipster, and always full of unexpected surprises. "Hawthorne" refers to a long stretch across Southeast Portland that culminates at Mt. Tabor Park. Take your pick of restaurants, both fine and lowbrow, before catching a movie at one of several old-style theaters. Or make an afternoon of it and wander the neighborhood's eclectic clothing boutiques and inviting bookshops in search of hidden treasure. Either way, you'll have a "keep Portland weird" experience.

INHALE DEEPLY
AT THE ROSE GARDEN

Portland isn't called the "City of Roses" for nothing. Throughout the summer, roses bloom aplenty in yards, parks, and highway medians around the area. But the real treat for your nose is the International Rose Test Garden, perched atop Washington Park. The aromas from every color, size, and shape fill the air, and the lookout over the city and Mt. Hood can't be beat (except, perhaps, at the Pittock Mansion, up the road). The place is massive, with more than 7,000 plants and 500 varieties—and test beds hold samples still being assessed for fragrance, color, and other attributes. The garden is free, and you also can meander through areas of 90-year-old prize winners and the shady Shakespeare Garden. There's no better place to pass a blissful summer afternoon on your own, with the family, or holding hands with a special someone.

400 SW Kingston Ave., Portland, OR 97205
503-823-3636
www.rosegardenstore.org

GET SPOOKED
IN THE SHANGHAI TUNNELS

Not so very long ago a world of crime and corruption was unfolding beneath our feet. In the early days of Portland's shipping business, underground tunnels linked the ports with the basements of hotels and other delivery destinations to limit street traffic and disruption. Rumors spread of drunken sailors who were lured underground and then shanghaied into service by unscrupulous captains. Today, companies lure tourists through these very same basements and brick archways with ghost stories and gimmicky displays. But there's also plenty of fascinating detail about the seedy underbelly of Portland in the late 1800s and early 1900s. The rotating door of tunnel tour companies will point out remnants of opium dens, illegal gambling rings, and gang hideaways. And whether or not you see a ghost, you'll definitely find that these underground lairs are a spooky place to hang.

CHEER ON
THE DRAGON BOATS
AT THE ROSE FESTIVAL

In a city that loves a good street fair, the Rose Festival is the
event to rule them all. You'll want to make an appearance at
the Grand Floral and Starlight Parades, but the festival lasts the
better part of a month. It's hard to miss the men and women
in uniform who roam the city during Fleet Week, and it's even
harder to miss the hulking military ships along the river. The
Dragon Boat Race is also a favorite: graceful boats, styled as
brightly colored dragons, compete along the Willamette River.
They're cheered on by members of the Rose Festival Court—
princesses and a queen culled from the Portland area's top high
school students. Throw in a carnival, live music performances,
great food, and lots and lots of flowers, and you've got yourself
a Rose Festival.

www.rosefestival.org

MEET PEGGY THE TRAIN
AT THE WORLD FORESTRY CENTER

Many visitors skip the World Forestry Center in favor of the higher-profile Zoo and Children's Museum, which sit just across the parking lot. But this unique little museum is worth a stop. The displays engage hands, eyes, and minds, and the larger exhibits lead guests along an in-depth adventure on the ecology, history, and geology of forests around the world. The center is rich with historic facts about the forestry industry in Oregon's early days, and you can pose alongside Peggy the Train, a 100-year-old locomotive that hauled over a billion feet of logs during the heyday of the Pacific Northwest logging industry. Modern exhibits include planting programs and forest fire management, and the upper level guides visitors through different types of forests from around the world. Don't forget to admire the inspired art displays featuring rotted wood, which is way cooler than it sounds, before heading out.

4033 Southwest Canyon Rd., Portland, OR 97221
503 228 1367
www.worldforestry.org

EXPLORE
NATIVE AMERICAN CULTURE

Before the region became known for gourmet donuts and heavily tattooed hipsters, hundreds of Native American tribes and communities thrived in the forests, mountains, valleys, coasts, and deserts of the Pacific Northwest. Today, nine sovereign Native American nations hold land in the state of Oregon, and the Portland area is home to members of dozens of First Nation communities. If you have the time, drive out to see one of the tribally owned reservation museums, like the Tamástslikt Cultural Institute. These centers give you a glimpse into the rich history and vibrant modern communities that thrive on reservations and throughout the state. In Portland, keep an eye out for powwows and events like the Jim Pepper Native Arts Fest, which shares authentic crafts, music, dancing, and culture with the greater Portland community. The Portland Art Museum is also known for its extensive collection of rare Native American artifacts and artwork.

Tamástslikt Cultural Institute
47106 Wildhorse Blvd., Pendleton, OR 97801
541-966-9748
www.tamastslikt.org

Jim Pepper Native Arts Festival
www.jimpepperfest.net

BE A HIPSTER
FOR A DAY

Which kind will you be? To the untrained eye, all hipsters can look the same. Creative, educated, liberal, young adults with plaid shirts and expensive eyeglasses, strong opinions on food and music, and a trust fund back in Connecticut in case that seven-hour-a-week bartending gig won't cover that kale smoothie habit. But the hipster experience is, in many ways, the Portland experience. Only the leisurely hipster lifestyle could support the delicious brunch options that abound across the city. The quirky, upstart bands and artists have created an unparalleled creative culture, and the hipster ideologies enable countless local businesses to flourish. So pick a day, sleep in, pull on your grandpa's old sports coat, and go to brunch with some friends on a Wednesday—just like a hipster.

RELAX
AT THE JAPANESE GARDEN

If the winter weather starts to wear you down, take an afternoon trip to the Portland Japanese Garden. When you're surrounded by its lush trees and trickling streams, the gray drizzle feels more like a cooling mist. After exploring the immaculately stylized ponds, stone gardens, and forests, you'll leave noticeably more Zen. Tucked away in Washington Park, this gem is a must-see for natives and tourists alike. There's an entrance fee, but once you're inside, the garden runs free tours throughout the day, and the guides are extremely knowledgeable about the plants, culture, and history of the garden. The waterfall is a Portland icon, and unique sculptures and carvings line the walkways. Tiptoe through the tea garden, wander over shady bridges, or participate in one of the many events it hosts throughout the year.

611 SW Kingston Ave., Portland, OR 97205
503-223-1321
www.japanesegarden.com

RIDE ALONG
ON A CITY BIKE TOUR

Grumbling drivers will warn you that Portland's streets are now for bikers first, cars second. They're right: we're consistently cited as one of the best cities in the country for bikes. Take advantage of this easy biking environment, and sign up for a bike tour of the city. Hop on your favorite two-wheeler (or three-wheeler if you prefer) or rent one from any of the many companies around the city. Your guide will cover more ground than a walking tour, but unlike a bus you'll still actually experience the city from the ground. Check out the options for specialty bike tours too: brewery rides, foodie rides, and local neighborhood adventures.

Pedal Bike Tours
503-243-2453
www.pedalbiketours.com

Brew Cycle
971-400-5950
www.brewgrouppdx.com/brewcycle

Cycle Portland
844-739-2453
www.portlandbicycletours.com

ATTEND A WORKSHOP
FOR DESIGN WEEK

You can't truly understand Design Week until you've been. The project is a collaboration between the city's creative visionaries. Architects, fashion influencers, graphic designers, and everything in between connect through workshops and art installations. Local businesses spread their doors for open houses and exhibits, and art installations pop up in some of the central neighborhoods. Interested in arts and crafts? There's an event for that. Curious about the latest in silicon forest design projects? The local design aesthetic runs strong, as does Portland's sports fashion culture. Immerse yourself in design thinking and take an entirely new look at the day-to-day items and amazing creative projects happening all across the city.

www.designweekportland.com

PAY A VISIT
TO BIG PINK

Portlanders have mixed feelings about Big Pink, a (mostly) affectionate name for the skyline's second-tallest building. The structure is officially known as US Bancorp Tower, but its nickname aptly describes the building's design, where Spanish granite along the façade is matched by pink-tinted reflective windows. Portland City Grill, one of the city's classic restaurants, offers stunning views from the 30th floor. The cooks serve delectable steaks and upmarket sushi to lucky diners as they gaze over the river and city lights and toward Mt. Hood, rising on the horizon.

111 5th Ave., Portland, OR 97204
503-450-0030
www.portlandcitygrill.com

GATHER
YE LAVENDER

The wayfaring Americans who followed the Oregon Trail were on to something, because the Pacific Northwest's fertile soil and temperate climate are ideal for farming. Pumpkins, apples, berries, and grapes grow aplenty. Among the mid-summer crops, you might encounter large swatches of purple lavender along the roadway. While you can buy bunches of the aromatic flowers and handmade oils, soaps, and culinary treats at farmers markets across the region, a trip to the countryside is worth the drive. Tour the farms, enjoy a perfumed U-pick session, or stop by one of the many festivals and events. Some of the farms serve up gourmet food and afternoon tea, so check websites for hours and details.

Find destinations and event listings at
www.oregonlavenderdestinations.com.

WALK ALBERTA STREET
ON LAST THURSDAY

The Alberta Arts District represents a perfect model of urban revitalization. The area in Northeast Portland, which was once run down and weary, decided to host a "Last Thursday" event that would be free to all artists, vendors, and performers. The program brought new life to the community, which now has block after block of vibrant local businesses. Take a walk down Alberta and you'll see vegan shoe shops, plus-size lingerie boutiques, art galleries, collectible book stores, quirky cafes, adventurous eating, and much more. And though the city has tried to normalize and organize Last Thursdays, the neighborhood has resisted the pull and remains open to any artists interested in participation. It's a fitting decision for a neighborhood that represents positivity and freethinking in the city's art community.

Northeast Portland, between NE 15th and 30th Avenues
along NE Alberta Street

GO WILD
AT THE OREGON ZOO

Entering the Oregon Zoo is like entering another world. No more skyscrapers, no more traffic. Though the cityscape is only a few short miles away, a walk around the zoo is a great way to escape. The beautiful and spacious exhibits have plenty of room for over 200 species and easy vantage points for curious guests. Take a walk down the wandering paths, and you might run into the beautiful giants in the elephant habitat. The park is particularly well known for its elephant breeding program, which supports the world's leading conservation programs. In the winter, ZooLights illuminates the forests and pathways. Admiring the colorful displays on cold winter nights has become beloved tradition for many a Portlander. The park also has its own MAX stop, and the entrance fee is reasonable, so you have no excuse not to visit.

4001 SW Canyon Rd., Portland, OR 97221
503-226-1561
www.oregonzoo.org

SHOPPING AND FASHION

TAKE A STROLL DOWN
NORTHWEST 23RD

In a city of trendy, cute neighborhoods, Northwest 23rd Avenue stands out by being a little trendier than the rest. Surrounded by blocks of stately, historic Victorian houses, 23rd itself is home to some of Portland's finest dining, drinking, coffee sipping, and shopping. Venture into some of the area's storefronts, which include high-end national brands, local specialty boutiques, and independent crafts stores. The area is lively any night of the week, but you can always take a walk and explore the quiet, hilly avenues of surrounding Nob Hill and the Alphabet District.

WALK THROUGH
THE STREET OF DREAMS

You may never own the finest house in town, but with Street of Dreams you can definitely walk through it. Every year, the city's best architects and designers team up to create a street of perfect houses. Firms vie for the opportunity to participate in the project, and the recognition is a peacock feather in the cap of any local builder. You can bet you'll see some stunningly innovative designs, and that those styles will be the benchmark for home décor for the following season. While the project generally works with new construction homes, keep an eye out for the occasional luxury remodel too. But be careful: explore these eye-boggling homes, and you may start dreaming of your own renovations and updates.

Late summer
www.streetofdreamspdx.com

LOOK THROUGH
THE RECORDS
AT MUSIC MILLENNIUM

The music industry has changed a lot in the last 50 years, but not Music Millennium. This independent record shop is crammed full of decades' worth of music. Hipsters and old-timers alike dig through the racks of vinyl, but you'll find plenty of CDs and DVDs to peruse as well. The range can be overwhelming to the casual music shopper. However, the staff is eager to help you track down long-retired no-name bands, or search for classics in great condition. The store throws an annual customer appreciation barbecue with music and food, and they regularly schedule in-store performances. A single visit to Music Millennium will convince you that vinyl is still alive and spinning.

3158 E Burnside St., Portland, OR 97214
503-862-8826
www.musicmillennium.com

CONQUER SUBURBIA
AT BRIDGEPORT VILLAGE

Located in one of the metropolitan area's most affluent communities (Tigard, for the curious), Bridgeport Village bills itself as an open-air "lifestyle center." This outdoor shopping space shocked the retail world when it opened in 2005 without an anchor store. Instead, its attractive, well-maintained walkways are lined with all the best high-end mall brands, convenient dining options, and family-friendly play areas. A stunning 18-screen theater and 3D IMAX are also attached. It's absolutely worth the drive from the city, if only to visit the most beautiful mall you'll ever see.

7455 SW Bridgeport Rd., #215, Tigard, OR 97224
971-276-8788
www.bridgeport-village.com

SHOP
VINTAGE

Shopping vintage is quintessentially Portland. It's environmentally friendly, guaranteed to leave you with quirky and one-of-a-kind looks to your wardrobe, and generally inexpensive. So it's no surprise that the vintage style scene here is competitive. While the influx of gentrifying hipsters has changed the second-hand retail industry in recent years, Portland's vintage market has never been stronger. Many shops are clustered along SE Hawthorne or in the less-restored parts of downtown, but you'll find hidden gems all across the city. Check out a few favorites.

Ray's Ragtime
A frequent stop for musicians, both A-list and indie,
performing in the city.
1001 SW Morrison St., Portland, OR 97205
503-226-2616

Avalon Antiques and Vintage Clothes
410 SW Oak St., Portland, OR 97204
503-224-7156

House of Vintage
3315 SE Hawthorne Blvd., Portland, OR 97214
503-236-1991
www.houseofvintageportland.com

WEAR GREEN
TO PORTLAND FASHION WEEK

Portland's status as an outré fashion hub has been growing for years. Much of it is inspired by the city's warped and clever street style and fertile art scene, and this small metropolis boasts more *Project Runway* winners than any other city. That "make it work" attitude has allowed Portland Fashion Week to quickly establish a niche for itself as one of the best indie fashion shows in the country and a leader in eco-friendly style. The project attracts designers of all ages and experience levels, who participate in couture, ready-to-wear, bridal, and special accessories shows. Billed as "the world's first carbon-negative fashion event," the entire production is sustained by solar power, fed locally sourced meals, and employs cruelty-free makeup and hair products. A partnership with the Art Institute of Portland attracts new local thinkers to the show, and you shouldn't be surprised if the styles you catch here are walking the streets of Milan next year.

www.portlandfashionweek.net

GET LOST
IN POWELL'S CITY OF BOOKS

Once you've passed through the doors, it's hard not to get lost at Powell's. This mecca of bookstores occupies multiple stories on an entire city block and is generally packed with people from all walks of life. Start wandering, and you'll get distracted in the dizzying rows until you find yourself in a back corner fully immersed in obscure science fiction titles, Mesopotamian art history, or carburetor repair manuals. The combination of new and used books means that the store rivals even top online retailers for selection and price, but Powell's also hosts readings and events with local and visiting writers. Pay a special visit to the rare book collection on the upper floor and the children's section, and then snag a table at the in-house coffee shop.

1005 W Burnside St., Portland, OR 97209
503-228-4651
www.powells.com

TIP
Feeling overwhelmed?
Ask for a color-coded map at the entrance to help guide you.

PAY A VISIT
TO ICON TATTOO

A guidebook should not be the reason you get a tattoo, but it should be the reason you learn a little more about this underappreciated art that has flourished in Portland for years now. No matter where you walk in Portland, you'll see unique tattoos: on young rebellious types, soccer moms, businessmen, even the elderly. Many people have more than one. Tucked just off of the Mississippi Avenue neighborhood in North Portland, Icon Tattoo's studio regularly attracts repeat customers. Its skilled team is responsible for walking works of art. If you're not in the mood to get inked yourself, take a peek inside the shop and admire the photos of their work. The staff is eager to answer questions, and you'll leave with a newfound respect for the art of tattoos.

813 N Russell St., Portland, OR 97227
503-477-7157
www.icontattoostudio.com

BUY SOMETHING WEIRD
AT THE SATURDAY MARKET

On weekend days, the Portland Saturday Market stretches several blocks west of the riverfront, where most visitors start their adventure. A seemingly endless collection of creators sell art, curious snacks and candies, and other wares in tented rows reminiscent of an old-world bazaar. Try the free samples, or feast on the pop-up food carts along the riverfront, and take your time rummaging through the artist creations. If you see a crowd circling off to the side, join them and catch jugglers, musicians, and performance artists hard at work. The Saturday Market is actually open all weekend, so you have no excuse for not checking out this Portland tradition.

2 SW Naito Pkwy., Portland, OR 97204
www.portlandsaturdaymarket.com

TIP
Hours and days vary seasonally,
so make sure to check the website before planning your visit.

SHOP
LIKE A BOSS

Portland, which often scoffs at both traditional sports and brand-name fashion, adores favorite son Nike. The company headquarters is just west of the city, in Beaverton, and employs thousands of people in the area. With so many staff, you'd think it would be fairly easy to get into the Employee Store, which is open only to Nike employees, their immediate families, and carriers of special passes. Not so: invites are few and far between. These golden tickets are highly coveted by athletes and fashionistas across the region. That's because the store sells both the sports staples and Nike's newest lines.

Nike Employee Store
3485 SW Knowlton Rd., Beaverton, OR 97005
503-671-1600
www.nike.com

The world's second-largest sportswear company, adidas, also maintains an awesome and exclusive company store available only to employees, their families, and those bearing special passes. The store lacks some of the mystique because the passes are easier to come by, but the rewards are the same, if not greater, and most shoppers binge on luxury sportswear at 50 percent off retail prices. Sponsor of a long roster of college, pro, and national-level sports teams around the world, adidas also offers a matchless supply of jerseys and gear for all of them, including the Timbers and Blazers.

adidas Employee Store
5060 N Greeley Ave., Portland, OR 97217
971-234-8536
www.adidas.com

Columbia Sportswear expresses itself as a passionately, proudly Oregonian brand, preparing adventurers for the wildest of Western adventures. The massive store near corporate headquarters sells, at varying discounts, nearly everything under the Columbia umbrella. Prana and Mountain Hardware hang alongside classic Columbia coats and clothes to provide a mix of rugged fashion, hardcore ski gear, and lumberjack plaids. Admission is limited to employees and ticketholders, and passes are limited, but not impossible to find.

Columbia Sportswear Employee Store
14100 NW Science Park Dr., Portland, OR 97229
503-985-4125
www.columbia.com

MUSIC, PIZZA, AND RECLAIMED HOMEWARES
ON MISSISSIPPI AVENUE

North Mississippi Avenue's revitalization is relatively new, and it has a lingering edginess that has long withered away in areas like the Pearl District. On Mississippi, the food carts are a little less polished, the tattoos are bolder, and the art is a little weirder. The street (along with neighboring Williams Avenue) has been buoyed by craft breweries and experimental restaurants, and the eclectic shopping options specialize in things like vintage construction materials, succulents, and handmade jewelry. Day and night, the neighborhood is busy with fascinating people to watch and meet. Be sure to check out Mississippi Studios, Mississippi Pizza, and the ReBuilding Center.

www.mississippiavenue.com

SUGGESTED
ITINERARIES

FUN WITH THE KIDS

Alpenrose, 20

Oregon Zoo, 110

Waffle Window, 37

OMSI, 93

Children's Museum, 76

Donuts, 12

Thorns, 56

iFLY, 63

HISTORIC PORTLAND

Huber's Café, 3

Hollywood Theatre, 49

Cathedral Park, 81

Shanghai Tunnels, 99

Native American Culture, 102

Portland Spirit, 58

VICE TOUR

FOODIE ELITE

HIPSTER

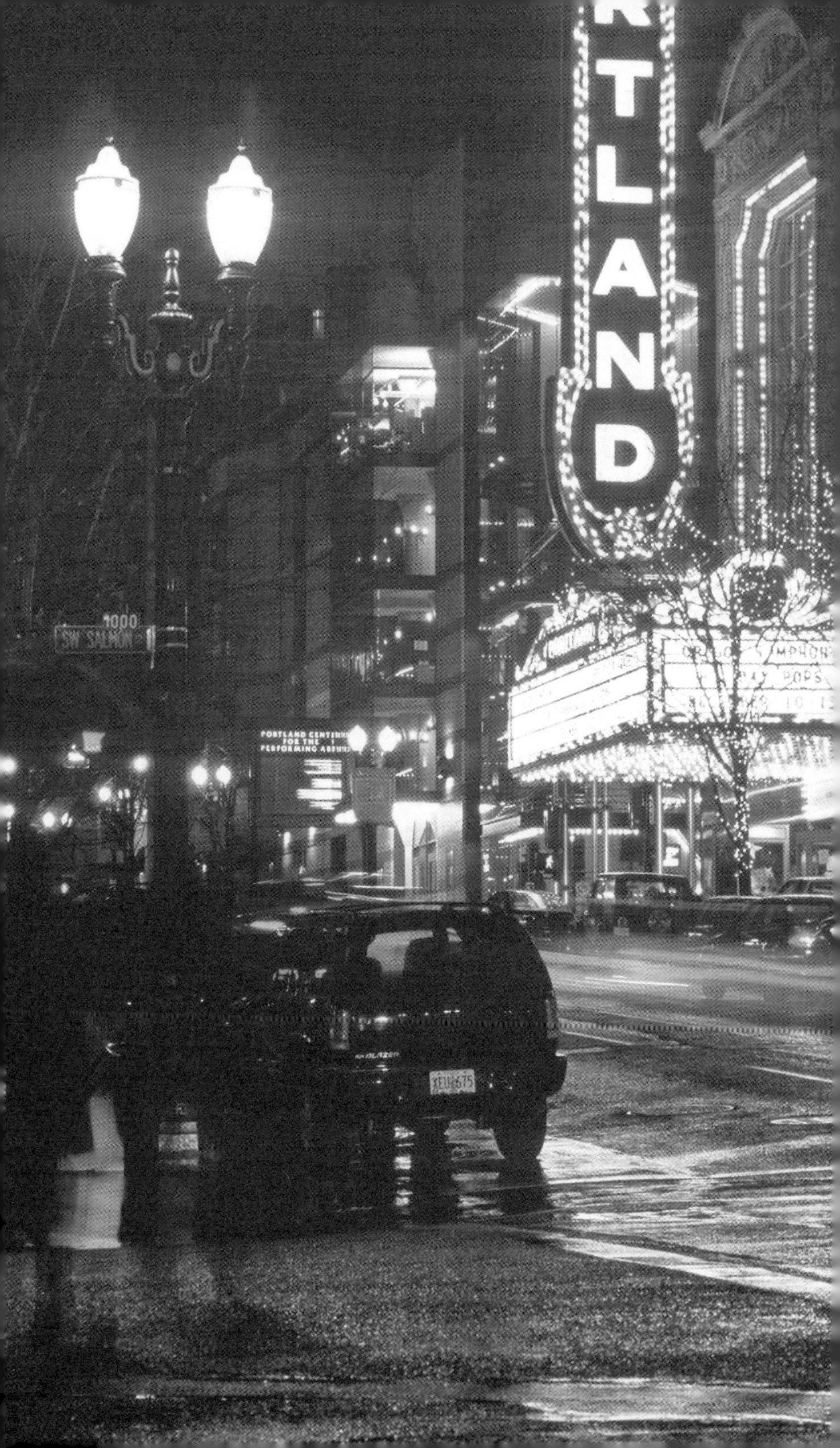
RTLAND
1000
SW SALMON ST
POPS

ACTIVITIES
BY SEASON

WINTER

Admire the Cows at Alpenrose, 20

Binge Watch *Portlandia,* 45

Ho Ho Ho Your Way to Santacon, 48

Cheer on the Portland Trail Blazers at a Home Game, 74

Ski the Slopes of Mt. Hood, 80

Oregon Zoo ZooLights, 110

SPRING

Celebrate St. Paddy's at Kells Irish Festival, 24

Get Some Instagram-Worthy Shots Along Tom McCall Waterfront Park, 75

Ride Along on a City Bike Tour, 105

SUMMER

FALL

INDEX